T0132419

In Life There Is a Way!

If You Believe

Ashleigh C'mone Smith

In Life There Is a Way!

If You Believe

iUniverse books may be ordered through booksellers or by contacting:

iUniverse
1663 Liberty Drive
Bloomington, IN 47403
www.iuniverse.com
844-349-9409

ISBN: 978-1-6632-4346-1 (sc)
ISBN: 978-1-6632-4345-4 (hc)
ISBN: 978-1-6632-4344-7 (e)

Print information available on the last page.

iUniverse rev. date: 09/21/2022

CONTENTS

Chapter 1: Oh No! My Sister Is Disabled

"Mommy, mommy, why is my sister not talking to me? Mommy, why is my sister in that big stroller? Hey Mommy, why are you feeding my sister? She's a big girl. Can't she feed herself?"

Yep, you got it right. These are all the questions that I didn't quite understand at four years old. You see, I was confused and full of questions. It wasn't until I was five years old that I thought, *Oh no! My sister is disabled.*

I'm not sure if you've ever heard of Rett syndrome, but it is a disorder that occurs mostly in girls, affecting their ability to talk, walk, and function properly. Some even have seizures, have difficulty breathing, and take lots of medications. I should know, because my sister was diagnosed with Rett syndrome. Truthfully, it is not easy to deal with at all.

So, you probably think that my sister is on a ventilator, has a tracheostomy tube and a feeding tube, and looks kind of weird. Well, that's where you're wrong! My sister, NaColby Jennings, is not on a ventilator and has neither a tracheostomy tube nor a feeding tube. Colby doesn't look weird either (not trying to be rude). Colby is very beautiful, smart, and fun to be around. However, my sister can't walk or talk, which is not easy to deal with for anyone. Nevertheless, I thank God that Colby doesn't have to take any medication, is still able to eat by mouth, and does not have seizures. My mom told me she used to have seizures when she was younger, but God healed her from them. I am glad that he did, because I don't know if I could have handled that part of her life. Then again, who knows?

- ***Inspirational Moment:*** It's very hard to have a family member with a disability. You must have patience and special love. I encourage people who have sisters or brothers like my sister to find a way to accept them the way they are, because they deserve love too. And God will bless you. Yes, it is hard, but in life, there is a way! I keep my faith and hope in the Lord, and each day becomes a better day. We are all faced with different challenges in life. Some may seem unbearable, but God will see you through. He never puts more on us than we can handle.
- Writing and exercising are the ways that I express my feelings about things. I encourage you to find positive ways to express your feelings as you face different challenges in life.
- Take time out for yourself and relax. It will get better if you believe.

Colby is an incredibly fun, cool, and unique sister to have. What makes Colby so cool and fun is that I get to make up all the rules, and she never complains. Another reason is that my sister never argues with me over who goes first. She laughs at all my jokes and keeps all my secrets to herself. Whenever I feel sad, she even rubs my face to let me know it will be OK. I love my sister and thank God for her every day. Colby's smile brings sunshine to a dark room.

However, I truly believe that if it weren't for our amazing mother, Deborah, Colby's life would be different. My mother is a strong, spiritual woman of God who refuses to settle for less. For example, my mother was told by someone (who I will not put on blast in this book) that she would not be able to make it with a disabled daughter. This person even told my mom that she would not be able to hold a nine-to-five job unless she put my sister in a facility. She was told that she might as well apply for government housing and accept the fact that her life was over. And even more crazy, she was told by someone else, whose name I won't disclose, that she needed to stay with Colby's dad, because no other man would deal with a child like that. That's mean, huh?

Well, some of it, my mom said, was a bit true. She said it was very difficult to hold a nine-to-five job with Colby. I still think that was mean for anyone to say, but my mom is the type that always finds the good in the bad.

Needless to say, lack of faith will hold anyone back. But my mom is a strong, determined woman of faith and perseverance who has a lot of vision. She is also very beautiful and smart, and I am not just saying that because she's my mom. It is true.

Deborah has proven to many people that having a daughter with a disability is even more reason to push harder. Regardless of what others say, don't let other people's fears interrupt your faith. My mom always quotes, "For I can do everything through Christ, who gives me strength" (Philippians 4:13, NLT).

My mom said it was difficult for her to accept that her firstborn wasn't a typical child. She wondered time and time again whether she had done something wrong. She told me that she isolated herself from a lot of family and friends, trying to figure it out and get away from all the questions and advice—"Is she talking yet?" "What's wrong with her?" "Is she walking yet?" "Put that girl behind the door and sweep her feet so she can walk." Crazy, huh? The nerve of some people. I see why my mom distanced herself. She would have gone crazy if she'd stayed around all that negative talk.

My mom says that it wasn't until Colby was three that she finally accepted that her firstborn was not able to talk or walk like normal kids. When she told me about this period, I could hear in her voice that it was very painful for her. My mom told me how she'd cried for many nights, trying to understand why. She'd even asked God why this had happened to her because she'd never drunk, smoked, done drugs, or done anything bad to cause harm during her pregnancy. She was angry and numb at first, but she never gave up on God. She knew that he never makes mistakes. She just needed answers as to why and how this had happened to her and her baby. Deborah had to bounce into reality so she could be good for Colby.

Once my mom realized that Colby was not going to be able to walk or talk, she had to learn how to care for Colby. My mom began to read books to help her understand how to care for a child with a disability. It wasn't easy at first, but we have all learned over the years that Colby is a true blessing to us all. So please remember that regardless of the fact that the person can't talk, he or she still loves it when you talk to him or her. I know, because Colby smiles every time we talk to her and keep her involved. It makes her very happy.

Colby communicates with her eyes by looking at what she wants and then looking at one of us. For example, if she is thirsty, she'll look at the cup and then at me. Then I'll say, "Colby, you want something to drink?" to let her know I am paying attention to her needs. She will then smile and look at the cup and then back at me again. That's when I give it to her to drink. Very cool, isn't it? The strange thing is that Colby knows how to hold her own sippy cup. I still haven't figured that part out.

Gaze is an incredible way for Colby to communicate with us. Let me tell you, Colby will even tell on you if you are doing something she doesn't like. For instance, I was trying to have a movie day with Colby in her room one day, but I wanted to watch a certain movie, and I guess she wanted to watch another movie. Well, when my mom came in the room, she told on me by making gestures and looking dead at me, frowning. My mom asked me what I'd done, and I said I hadn't done anything. But Colby kept on with the sounds and looking at me. So, I got in trouble and had to turn the TV to what Colby wanted to watch. Do you know she actually laughed at me? Yes, I said she laughed. Just because she can't talk doesn't mean she doesn't have a personality.

* * *

Creating a fulfilling life for my sister has not been easy, but my mom has done an amazing job at it. She has always made sure Colby is happy and comfortable wherever we go. We are a very close family that does everything together. We take my sister out every weekend to have some fun. She mostly loves going to the movies and out to eat. I decided to call these excursions Colby's weekend getaways. Colby has also gone on many vacations to the beach and even flown first class!

Moment of Expression

Sometimes I feel bad for my sister, because I don't know what she is really thinking when she sees everybody moving around doing things and she can't. I don't want her to ever feel like she is forgotten about or missing out on things, so I started this thing called "sissy night." I've been doing this since I was six years old and Colby was sixteen, and she enjoys every bit of it. I also include her in some things with my friends. Most of my friends accept my sister for who she is and act like Colby is their friend too, which makes Colby and me feel special.

Everybody, including family, says that when I came into Colby's life, I turned on a light bulb in her, because I am the little/big sister Colby looks up to. There is never a dull moment with us—unless she is telling on me!

Ashleigh Smith (that's me! Colby's little eleven-year-old sister) is the most caring, loving, and kind person—at least that is what everyone tells me. My mom's friends love to see how I care for Colby. They get emotional seeing that as young as I am, I care for my sister with such passionate love. Well, I feel like my sister needs me, and if God placed me in her life, I must do my best to care for her. Plus, I honestly really love and care about my sister.

- *Inspirational Moment:* I encourage anyone who has a sibling with a disability not to give up on him or her. I understand that it is hard. There are days when it is hard physically, emotionally, and mentally. It is even hard sometimes when making new friends; you wonder what they will think about you having a sibling with a disability. But know this: real friends understand and accept you the way you are. They don't judge you or make fun of you for having a disabled sibling. Truthfully, there are people in the world who say mean things but pay them no attention. God will deal with them. So, keep your head up. God does not put more on us than we can handle. You were born for this, and in life, you will find a way! My mom gave me several Bible scriptures to post on my bathroom mirror. One of my favorites is Psalms 28:7 (NIV): "The Lord is my strength and my shield; my heart trusts in him, and he helps me. My heart leaps for joy, and with my song, I praise him."

God Made Me This Way

God has blessed our lives in a unique way by giving us Colby. Some people who lack spiritual understanding believe that having a child with a disability is a curse; not me, not now or ever. I know my sister's life is a blessing from God. It has taught me to have patience, unconditional love, more passion for others, and more faith. You see, we have faced many challenges in my family having Colby in our lives, but we always find a way to make it work. My mom told me about the times when she was stuck with me (as a baby) and Colby (in a wheelchair) at the same time and needed to go to the store. Now, can you imagine shopping with a child in a wheelchair and an infant? Well, she made it work. She invented a swinging carriage to put me in that she could attach to Colby's wheelchair in such a way that it was as though Colby were holding me. And it worked! She says it worked so well that she started taking us for walks in the neighborhood like that. I wonder why she never tried to pitch the idea on *Shark Tank*. Prayer and love have a big impact on our family. It is the best part of what keeps us happily together!

- *Inspirational Moment:* I believe that God put me in my sister's life to help inspire others and show that his work is not finished. Just when you think it is, he'll show you it's just starting. So, I've always told myself to never give up on God, because he does things for a reason. And when things happen in your life, never wish they were happening to somebody else, because you would only be wishing your own blessings away.
- When it gets hard, I ask God to help me. And trust me, he always does.

OK, I've Got to Say This

To all the people out there reading this book who told my mom she could not make it through life with a disabled daughter or knew she needed help but refused to help her, just look at Deborah Booze now. She is a successful business owner. My mom took her pain and sorrow from having a disabled child and turned it into a ministry. When people ask me who my role model is, I have to say my mom. She not only carries herself as a godly woman, but she has earned many degrees and is a few months away from having her PhD. Go, Mommy! Do you want me to keep going?

What I'm really trying to say is that my mom made it, even though people said she wouldn't, and that's what I love about my mom. She's always worked hard for what she wanted and never gives up, even if she wants to. I know what you're probably thinking: how did Deborah make it? Well, lucky you. I have the inside story. My mom is a true believer and a hard worker.

When I was younger, I would be in my mom's room with her every night before going to bed, and she would be reading her Bible. I would hear her praying over all of us and even praying for everyone else in the world. I've always told myself that I want to be like her and trust that God is always there for me. I want to have the same faith that she has that God will never leave me alone.

Having Colby as my sister has taught me that you should always be yourself. Basically, don't feel insecure about how you look or feel, because no matter what, there are going to be people who are not always kind in the world. We are all made in the image of God; therefore, we are uniquely made in some way.

I've learned from my sister to enjoy life. My mom always says, "Live life and laugh a lot," so I've decided that in life, that is what I will do. Colby always has a smile on her face, although she can't do anything for herself. Seeing that amazing smile on her face teaches me not to complain about little things and not to mope around and act sad just because things are not going my way. She also taught me patience, because Colby must wait for us to do everything for her and usually doesn't complain.

Could you imagine having to wait for someone to put you on the toilet or bring you a glass of water when you are thirsty? What about having to wait for someone to bring you a snack when you are hungry or even turning the TV to another channel when you are tired of watching *SpongeBob SquarePants*? I had to add that in because that's one of the few times when Colby complains. Television is her favorite, and she absolutely runs the whole house when it comes to what she wants to watch. You should see us playing the guessing game:

"What, Colby? Mickey Mouse?"

Colby looks at us with distress.

"No?" We turn to *Wonder Pets!* "You want to watch this?"

Colby again looks and moans.

"No?"

Finally, after five tries, we get it: *Backyardigans*. We find that hilarious, because she now knows that she is in control of something, and that makes her feel like the boss.

Chapter 2: The Pain of Saying Goodbye to My Dad

Phone rings.

Me: Hey, Daddy!

Dad: Hey, what are you doing?

Me: Nothing. What are you doing, Daddy?

Dad: Nothing much.

Me: Oh, OK! Can't wait to see you this summer!

Dad: Me too. Maybe we can go to the water park!

Me: Yeah!

We talk for a few more minutes, and then my dad has to go.

Dad: OK, Call you later, baby girl, Love you!

Me: OK, Daddy. Love you too.

I hang up the phone.

Summer was finally here. What an exciting time of my life. I didn't mention this, but my mom and dad got a divorce when I was six years old. I had been really mad at first, but then I'd realized that I had no reason to be mad. My mom never kept me away from seeing my dad when I wanted to. Plus, my mom and my dad, Lucious Smith, actually got along like best friends after their divorce.

My dad and I FaceTime each other every day. You see, once they'd gotten a divorce, my dad had moved back to Georgia, while we'd stayed in Virginia.

My dad had started dating this nice lady, and my mom had gotten remarried when I was nine years old to Tredrick Booze Sr, who is known as Double, a man I think is the coolest dad on earth besides my biological dad.

Anyway, moving along.

What was so great about this summer was that we got an RV that slept six to eight people, and we were going to be camping in the RV for ten long days. We all packed our things and headed to Georgia. My mom and stepdad had agreed to spend the Fourth of July with my dad at the campground. It was going to be a big family reunion for us all!

I knew this Fourth of July was going to be better than the last ones! We had people from both my mom's side of the family and my stepdad's side of the family coming down to the park to join us. And of course, people from my dad's side of the family came too. Yes, I said my dad's family. As I mentioned earlier, my mom and dad got along like family. That's what I love most about my parents. They taught me how two people can still love each other and not be together. I pray that more parents take on that attitude for their kids.

So, we were on the way to Georgia. We stopped and grabbed some lunch. I had never been so excited to see my daddy. While we were on the road, the RV was full of the sound of music, the TV, and phone calls from my dad.

I could tell my dad was just as excited as I was. He kept calling me every hour to see how far away we were and if we were OK.

When we got there, I spent the first few days at my dad's place so I could spend some time with him, while Colby and my mom and stepdad, which I call Daddy-double (now that I like him), camped in the RV together behind my dad's apartments until it was time to go to the campground.

Well, as always, my dad kept his promises.

The day after we got there, my dad and his fiancée took her daughter and me to the water park, and it was so much fun.

Four days later, my mom and Daddy-double left to go to the campsite, while my sister and I stayed with my daddy for a few more days. My daddy was like a daddy to Colby too. He had been in her life since she'd been four years old. We watched movies, played games, and ate food. Colby and I both enjoyed hanging out with my dad. After all those days of fun, my mom called me and said that she was going to come to pick us up. They had gotten a rental car to drive, so they didn't have to haul that big RV around everywhere. We would hang out at the campsite so we could have fun at Stone Mountain and go to the shows.

The next day was the Fourth of July, and the big reunion was about to begin. They had put up three tents. We had a karaoke machine, music, a video camera, tables, chairs, fans, and lots of delicious food. Everybody was having a great time laughing, eating, drinking, talking, and singing. The young people all went to the swimming pool while the food was being prepared. Boy, was that fun.

I know this might sound crazy, but my mom and my dad's fiancée got along well, just like Daddy-double and my dad got along like brothers. The rest of the family was amazed at how they were hanging out in the kitchen, talking and laughing together, but I wasn't. I just knew that my mom and my dad's fiancée were true examples of godly women.

* * *

I kept going over to check on my dad to make sure he was OK and see if he needed anything, because it was super hot outside. I, of course, was a daddy's girl.

You are probably wondering how I could have been a daddy's girl when all I have talked about in the book so far has been my mom. Well, you see, they are both wonderful parents. My mom is my inspiration to do right in life, work hard at whatever I do, never give up, stay connected to Christ, get my education, and more, while my dad treated me like his little princess. So, I got the best of both worlds.

Back to what I was saying.

I know you are wondering why I was checking on him. My dad struggled with diabetes for years, along with other medical conditions. It had gotten so far out of control that he'd had to have some parts of his limbs amputated. Even though my dad suffered from a lot of pain, he would always try to make his kids happy by playing games with us.

I often wondered when I was younger why, if God has all power to do whatever, he hadn't made my sister able to walk and talk and had not cured my dad's diabetes. There were many nights I would lie in my bed crying, talking to God about these things. That was a secret that no one knew. I was mad, sad, confused, and somewhat tired of it all. I wondered whether anyone else out there in the world felt like me or even had a dad and sister who were disabled. I felt like I'd gotten a raw deal out of life. By the time I'd been born, my dad had already had his toes amputated. Later, he had to have half his left foot removed. It was crazy to see him sitting without a shoe on. Just imagine what that looked like for me. But it was part of what my dad had to go through in life—or rather what he'd put himself through.

My mom told me that before I was born, the doctor had told my dad that if he didn't make some life changes by improving his diet and exercising, then by the time I was born, he would not be able to run around with me. Well, the doctor was right. An elderly lady also told my mom that if my dad didn't get it together, by the time he was 40, my mom would be a widow. It was hard for my dad to move around, but he did the best he could. So, for that, I love him even more. I admired my dad a lot.

I had such a great time that summer with my family that it seemed too good to be true. I would never have thought we would all be together like that in a million years.

I had a great time with my dad and my family, but little did I know that it would be the last summer—the last time—I would ever spend time with my dad.

You're probably like, *What!* Yep, that was the last time.

Inspirational Moment: Life is only a moment. Life is to be lived while you have it, for in a moment, it could be gone. So, love to live, learn how to forgive, and remember you are not alone when someone you love is gone, for life is for a moment!

Two months after our trip, my best friend, Nipa, invited me to go to this pumpkin patch place with her, and I said sure. First, though, I had to ask my mom. My mom said yes, I could go. Nipa and I had been friends since I'd been in second grade. Nipa and her mom were the only people my mom trusted me to hang out with without her being with me. I was excited about going. I knew it was late, but like always, I called my dad and told him about it.

Phone rings.
Daddy: Hello!
Me: Hey, Daddy. Whatcha doing?
Daddy: Hey, baby girl. Watching TV. What are you doing?
Me: Daddy, my friend asked me to go to the pumpkin patch with her in the morning.
Daddy: What did your momma say?
Me: She said I could go. I can't wait, Daddy.
Daddy: Well, you better get you some rest. Love you.
Me: OK, Daddy. Love you too. I'll call you in the morning. Good night.

Earlier that day, I had gotten some rubber bands so I could make bracelets. While I was talking to my dad, I asked him if he wanted one, and he said sure. I asked him what colors he wanted his bracelets to be, and he said red and blue, because those were his two favorite colors. I told my dad that I would give it to him the next time I saw him or next summer, and he agreed.

The next day, my dad called me and woke me up, reminding me that I had to go to the pumpkin patch that day.

I woke up, got dressed, and called my dad back. While I was talking to him on FaceTime, Nipa called and said she was in front of my house.

So, I told my dad that I would call him when I got home and that I loved him, and he was like, "OK, have fun. Love you too."

While I was at the pumpkin patch, my head started to hurt severely. It hurt so badly that I started crying. Nipa's mom kept asking me if I was OK. I told her my head was hurting really badly. So, we stopped and got food. She thought that being out in the sun and not eating was probably why my head was hurting.

My mom is always getting on me for not eating as I should.

When I got home, my mom was upset, because she knew I'd left without eating.

You see, my family believes in having breakfast, lunch, and dinner. And not only do we believe in it, but we also sit at the table as a family and eat together. I love that, because we get to talk with each other about our days.

Back to what I was talking about. I hadn't eaten the food my mom had told me to eat before I'd left, so when she got on me, I started crying again. I went upstairs to my room and took a nap, because my head was hurting severely for some reason that day.

When I woke up from my nap, I called my dad, because I was still upset from my mom getting on me and Daddy always knew what to say to make me feel better.

But he didn't answer.

So, I called again, and again, and he didn't answer.

Usually, he would have answered by now. You see, my dad was disabled, so he didn't work. Nor did he do much away from home. So, I kept calling until this guy answered the phone. I didn't know who he was by listening to his voice, but he knew my name.

He said, "Hello, Ashleigh."

I kept quiet.

Then he said, "Where is your mommy?"

So, I ran to give the phone to my mommy. She was in the kitchen getting something for Colby to drink.

I stood right beside her, waiting to see who it was, but I couldn't hear anything.

Then I saw this weird look on my mom's face, and she ran out the front door. You can imagine me standing there, already confused about who this guy was answering my dad's phone. I got scared and went into the room with my sister. In fact, I was so nervous and scared that I threw up.

My mom was still outside. I still didn't know what was going on. I thought that maybe, if I went back upstairs to my room, I could look out my window to try to see what my mom was talking about, but that didn't work. The only thing I could see was that something must be wrong; my mom looked like she was crying out there.

A few minutes passed, and then I heard Daddy-double's phone ring. So, I ran to my doorway, listening to see if it was my mom who had called him. (Our bedrooms were across from one another—well, sort of. The stairway was between our rooms.) But I saw Daddy-double run down the stairs in fear.

OK, let's stop right there. So, this is how I knew something was wrong with my dad, because if my stepdad runs down the stairs and is showing some type of emotion, like fear, then you know something is going on. But let's get back to the story. I rushed back to my window. Now my stepdad was standing outside with my mom, hugging her, and my mom was standing there crying.

After about thirty minutes, my mom and Daddy-double came back into the house. I rushed downstairs. At that time, my mind was elsewhere. All I was thinking was, Where is my dad? What is going on? Why is my mom crying? And who was that man who answered my dad's.

I didn't know how to feel, especially when my mommy told me to go upstairs and wait in my room for a minute and said she would be right there. My body went numb. I was very nervous. All I was thinking was, *Where is my dad?*

Now, there I was in my room, and my mom came and sat on the bed with me. I could tell that whatever my mom was about to say, it was not going to be good. I can remember it like it just happened.

My mom looked me in the eyes and said, "Ashleigh, baby, the time has come. Your dad has gone to heaven to be with the Lord."

It took me about two or three minutes to figure out what she was saying to me. I'd known what she was going to tell me wasn't going to be good, but I'd never expected it to be that my dad was gone!

I burst into tears: my dad, my best friend, my world.

I just couldn't take it anymore. I felt like I wanted to give up on everything and everyone!

But as soon as I felt like that, the strangest thing happened. The Holy Spirit came to me. Honestly. It was a feeling I'd never felt before. It was so surreal but true. Then Jesus spoke to me and said, "Now your dad is way better than he has ever been. He is safe with me now." I just held on tight to my mom in silence. At that moment, I realized that life is just a moment. Live life while you can, for in a moment, it could be gone. Forgive and love and remember that you are not alone. (Everyone always told me I had an old soul. I guess that's why I thought the way I did about things and was more advanced than others in my age group.)

My mom said I could stay home for the week or as long as I needed to from school. It sure was different in my house. My whole routine had to change. Every morning, my dad had called to wake me up for school. We would talk for a few minutes, and then he'd tell me he loved me and tell me to have a good day at school. Those calls were very special to me and really made my day. And after school, I couldn't wait to FaceTime my dad and tell him how my day had gone. He would even help me with my homework when my mom was busy with her nursing school, or Daddy-double was cooking dinner. Colby was just as connected as I was to my dad, if not more, because he had been in her life since she was four years old. I would always go downstairs to Colby's room so he could talk to her on FaceTime. Colby would smile so wide. She loved my dad very much.

The next day, my mom and Daddy-double tried to keep me busy by taking me out to breakfast and the mall. Even though I enjoyed it, I was just sad and missing my dad. If only I could have heard his voice one more time.

Now I get it. The Lord knew that that was the day for my dad to come home to him, so he'd had my friend keep me occupied and keep me from calling my dad or even being on the phone with him when he passed away.

You see, the guy on the phone was my dad's cousin, my older cousin Cee. He'd found my dad facedown on the floor of his apartment unconscious. That morning, when I had talked to my dad on the phone, he'd told me that he wasn't feeling too well and that he was getting dressed to go out to the store. Then, my friend called me on the other line to let me know they were out front, so I had to go. I found out later that when my dad's cousin had found him, my dad was still putting on his pants when he'd collapsed facedown on the floor.

I just couldn't imagine having been on the phone with my dad when that had happened. So, yes, I know that God had my friend call me just in time. That would have been very hard for me if I had to hear my dad dying while I was on the phone with him. How helpless and painful that would have been for me. Then I questioned myself, that if I was on the phone, maybe I could have called for help. This is something I will never know (in a sad voice).

After the fourth day of not going to school, I told my mom that I was finally ready to go back. My mom was still very concerned about how I would do returning to school, so she came to have lunch with me that day. My mom had also told all my teachers that my dad had passed away to explain my absence from school.

Later that school day, the most amazing thing happened to me: there was a white envelope on my desk with my name on it. I didn't open it while I was at school but instead waited until I got back home. It said, "Sorry for your loss," and all my teachers had written a little message for me inside. It was so sweet, and it made my heart warm. I started crying, but this time it was different. I was now accepting that my dad was happy and healthy in heaven. And because of that, I felt better.

A little background on my parents' relationship: My mom, Deborah, and my dad, Lucious Smith, were married for eleven years. Then my dad moved to Atlanta to live his life, and my mom, my sister, and I stayed in Virginia. As I mentioned before, my mom and dad remained great friends. My dad came to almost every event we had. My mom would even surprise me and bring my dad to the school, where we would all have lunch together. He would catch a flight here from Atlanta. Oh boy, those were some exciting moments. But once I got older, my mom started to take me to visit my dad every other month. My dad got a new place in Atlanta and met this girl named Grace Cowell. She became my dad's new girlfriend. At first, I thought that maybe she would be mean to me, but then I realized that she was really nice. I could tell that my dad loved her, so I started to think of her as a stepmom.

Then one day, my dad called me and asked me if it would be OK if he married Ms. Grace, and I said yes, that Ms. Grace is nice. He said OK and asked me if I was sure he could marry her. I was like, yes! You see, that is the kind of relationship my dad and I had. I was his little princess, and he wanted to be sure if anyone was going to be in his life that I was OK with it and that she treated me right.

So, my dad called my mom and told her that he was going to marry Ms. Grace. He wanted to know her thoughts too. I thought that was cute, my dad asking my mom's opinion about somebody he wanted to marry. My mom was so happy for him and told him to go for it. (Just a reminder: they were the best of friends. They should've been able to tell each other this kind of stuff.) My dad even called Daddy-double and told him, because they were good friends also.

Unfortunately, my dad died, and he never got the chance to marry Ms. Grace. My dad's passing actually made me start opening up more to my mom. I had always talked to her, but it was different not having my dad's opinion on things.

My mom told me after my dad's death that she was so proud of me because I never gave up on God. She told me she knew my dad was someone so dear to me.

I still pray and thank God for everything and every day. Now, I would be lying if I said I didn't miss my dad, because I do. But I try to move on with my life and not be sad, because I know that my dad wouldn't want that. When he was here, he always made me happy, and now that he is looking down at me, I know he still wants the same for my life. He always wanted me to make good choices in life and to be successful at whatever I did. So, that is what I try to do. Besides, my mom won't accept me not doing the right thing.

At just eleven years old, I had accomplished quite a bit in life. (Yes, my dad passed when I was only eleven years old.) But I do wonder what life would be like now if my dad were still alive. Like, I wonder what he would say about me having my own T-shirt printing company.

Chapter 3: The Mental and Emotional Stress of Having a Sick Dad

My life has always revolved around caring for my dad or my sister, but this part is about my dad. You see, I always worried about my dad, even more, when my mom and dad got a divorce. I felt like I was responsible for making sure he was OK. I believe that was a big part of why I was on the phone with him for almost 24-7. My dad had to take insulin twice a day. He would get dizzy quite often, because he didn't eat when he should, and because he struggled with keeping his blood sugar level controlled. I worried and prayed for my dad all the time. I wanted all of this to go away. I wanted my dad to get his limbs back. And I wanted him to be healthy again.

I'm pretty sure you want to know what caused my dad to get sick: diabetes! It is a nasty monster that takes over your body if you don't take it seriously.

Diabetes is a condition where the pancreas produces very little insulin, a hormone required for the body to use blood sugar. My dad had diabetes way before I was even born, and yet it still affected me. That was because I really wanted to enjoy a lot of things with my dad, but he couldn't do everything, like chase me in the park, race me on a track, teach me to ride a bike, or go bike riding with me. My brother wanted to play football with Dad. I wanted to go on rides at water parks and go swimming. I wanted to go on roller coasters. I wanted him to be able to come to visit me whenever, but he couldn't drive long distances. There were so many more things.

Although it may seem like I was ungrateful for my dad because he was not able to do those things with me, I was not!

My dad was the best dad in the world, and he was secretly my favorite. I mean, I love my mom and stepdad too, but my mom has always been the strict parent while my dad was more silly and fun. There's a big difference between the two. My dad always tried to do what he could for me, Colby, and my big brother, Elijah, to make us happy. (Elijah is my half-brother, my dad's son from before my parents got married. He is almost four years older than me.)

My dad tried the best he could. I saw how it bothered him that he wasn't able to do certain things with us. I think that is why my dad pushed hard to do the things he did. For example, I will never forget when my dad took me to the subway station. I know that it was a lot for him. We had to keep stopping for him to rest. I felt terrible, but he insisted on taking me so that I could have the experience of riding on the subway.

Sometimes, he let me put makeup on him and paint his nails. Now, that was really funny and fun. He would even try to get up and dance with us. My dad was such a great dad. Even with his amputations, he attempted to run with my brother and me. He would call his best friend to come to pick us up to go across town just to get ice cream. These were little moments of my life that will never be forgotten.

I used to sit and watch my dad put his wrap around his foot. As I recall, he'd had half of his foot amputated, which means that he'd had part of his foot removed. I felt so sorry for my dad. It looked very painful. I wanted to help, so I would hand him his gauze, tape, and bandage. I felt like a little nurse with my gloves on helping him. I used to tell my mom that when I graduated, I was going to move to Atlanta to take care of my dad. My mom would just smile and say, "OK, Ashleigh, I hear you."

So, let's talk about this for a minute. My dad had both of his feet partially amputated, so it was hard for him to keep his balance. But he still stayed strong for his kids. People said at the time that my dad should have died a long time ago. He developed diabetic ketoacidosis (DKA) multiple times, from what my mommy told me. That is when a person goes into a coma, because his or her diabetes is out of control. All I remember is always going to the hospital to visit him.

It was sometimes scary for me to watch him get up and struggle just to walk on two feet. It's very painful. Many nights, I cried thinking about what would happen if something happened to my dad. I never wanted my mom and dad to know this, but I was always afraid of getting that call, because my dad lived alone, and I had seen for myself how hard it was for him to get around some days.

I would always ask my dad, Did you take your medicine? What you eat, Dad? I think it got on his nerves sometimes, but he never told me if it did.

My dad never really talked about his pain, but I saw it in his face and heard it in his voice. This was hard for me as a child. Seeing my dad suffer like that made me sad, because the reality was, there was nothing I could do but pray. So, I prayed for my dad so much. I just wanted him to be better.

As crazy as this may sound, even though my sister is also disabled, there truly was a big difference between her and my dad. You can't even compare the two, because truthfully, I have never really seen my sister in pain. She is always happy and smiling. I thank God and my family for that. You know what I think? I really think my sister is an undercover angel that God put here on earth to see how the people in her life would treat her. The ones who treat her well are blessed, and the ones who overlook her miss out on the blessing. There's a story in the Bible that talks about God's angels. I think Colby is one.

I am blessed to have her as my sister

Back to the topic, my dad had high cholesterol too. Cholesterol is a waxy, fatlike substance that the body needs to function normally, but too much cholesterol is bad. Eating certain foods, like fried chicken, french fries, and other fried foods, can cause high cholesterol, and my dad loved this stuff very much. We are not going to get into that topic as much, though, because I don't know how much it really affected my dad. So, on to the next topic!

My dad also had high blood pressure, which is when the force of your blood pushing against the walls of your blood vessels is consistently too high. So basically, my dad had to check his blood pressure and blood sugar every day. That was a lot, especially for my dad, because he loved his fried chicken. So, you know where this is going: that fried chicken was hard to let go of.

I miss my dad!

Inspirational Moment: God reminds us that even at the most challenging times of our lives, he is with us. Life has its ups and down, but I have learned that the word of God is my strength. I wake up every morning and pray before I start my day. Taking time to do what matters most is how you find a way in life to get things done or accept the things you cannot change. You see, even when we are faced with the most difficult times of our lives, we must always turn to the word of God, for he is our strength. He will comfort us and guide us until we find peace with it all. I know. I tried it for myself, and it works. Please, if you have lost anyone close to you in life, I encourage you to find strength in prayer. And if you don't know how to pray, find a family member or friend, and ask that person to pray with you.

I'll share with you a little prayer, hoping that I can help one soul in the time of sorrow and that one day, you will be able to say, "Now I can bless another soul that faces the same kind of sorrow":

Dear Lord, I am hurting and angry too.
Yet I'm helpless and lonely without a clue.
My heart is pain; I can't even explain.
I lost my friend, my dad (put the name here); my lifelong friend is gone,
And I feel all alone.
So here I am, Lord; it's just me and you. I'm trusting you to give me strength to see it through.
I need your comforter and your guidance too.
I need your love to hold me close.
Lord, please come quick to fill this hole, and dry my face from all the rain,
For only you can help a dear child like me
Recover from all this pain.
So, I thank you, Lord, now for hearing my prayer and
For making each day get better along the way as I pray.
Amen!

Chapter 4: Making My Mom and Stepdad Proud

I love my mom so much, and she loves me so much more. Making my mom proud is not that hard, as long as I listen, follow directions, and do the right thing. My mom wants so much for me in life, and if I want it too, I have to work to get it. You see, I am not bragging or anything, but I have a pretty good lifestyle with my family. My mom has always been a go-getter. Ever since I was born, my mom has had her own business. So, she has been my biggest inspiration. Even though I already have my own T-shirt printing company, I plan to go to law school and become an attorney. My goal is to successfully have my own law firm. Let's see, the *Law firm of Ashleigh Smith and Associates.* Sounds good to me. However, the week after my daddy passed away, I did tell my mom that I wanted to be an actor. You see, I've always had it in me. I have been writing plays since I was five years old. I would get all my friends over to play characters in my plays. I have also written several short stories that my mom keeps in her filing cabinet. As you can see, this one got away and into the hands of a publisher (in my laughing voice).

All of a sudden, after I mentioned wanting to act to my mom, she saw an ad announcing auditions for this TV show for children. She emailed the production group, and what do you know, I got a call to come in for the audition.

My school life was always very important to my mom and me, so she would never put anything over my education. She always tells me that she wants me to be smarter than her and ten times better than her at whatever I do. I have the best mommy!

One of the things that she says to me all the time is, "If you can believe it, then you can achieve it." So, I started believing that I could be anything I wanted to be, such as a dancer, writer, actress, attorney, or singer. Shoot, one day, I might have my own film-production company.

I love the way my mom has instilled in me the desire to always trust in God and never give up She even gave me a daughter affirmation to hang in my bathroom for me to read every day. It has been with me for four years now. I would like to share it with you.

My Life Affirmation

Today I stand taking full charge over my life. I have and always will put Jesus first in all I do. And because I am his precious child, I know that I am the head, and not the tail.

He has created me with boldness, beauty, confidence, intelligence, and a creative mind. I am my father's masterpiece, and no good thing is withheld from me.

I am protected and covered by the blood of Jesus wherever I go. I understand in order to be what I want to be in life, I must work hard, be dedicated, and self-motivated. Therefore, I will not let the things, nor people, around me distract me from my destiny.

I will face any challenge put before me with God's help to overcome it; I will rebuke anything that tries to discourage me along the way, for quitting is not an option, and cheating is not an alternative.

I understand for me to show good stewardship, I must withhold characteristics that edifies loyalty, reliability, honesty, faithfulness, respect,

loving, caring, and kindness. I must also show myself as a person with integrity and dignity.

I will keep in mind that not everyone who smiles at me, is for me. Therefore, I will continue to pray for guidance and a spirit of discernment. I will not be afraid to try new things, or go new places, if it is in the plan that God has for life.

I am excited about my success and know that I can do all things through Jesus Christ who strengthens me. I will accomplish many goals in my youth, and the wealth that my father has left on earth for me I will inherit at a young age. I am blessed, I am favored, and I am my father's masterpiece.

—Deborah Booze

My mom and stepdad are great together. They pray together and with me and my sister. We have family talk practically every day. I love it. Mom makes me read my devotion every morning. Well, she used to make me read, but now I do it on my own. It really helps me a lot. I know I haven't said much about my stepdad, but, boy, is he the coolest and most caring person to be around. We have so much fun together.

You see, my stepdad retired from the navy. He is also a very smart guy. He got his master's in business management, so he helps with my mom's business. But truly, if you let me tell it, I think Daddy-double really wanted to be a rapper. He is forever freestyling to music and dancing.

One day, I caught him off guard. I had written a short rap and shared it with him and my mom. You know where this is going. My stepdad ended up remixing my lyrics and making it his own. Being around him kind of got me out of being shy, and I started freestyling with him a lot more. That's another one of my little talents that I keep hidden. We'll battle back and forth with each other, and my mom and Colby will be the judges. I enjoy every moment of it.

We are a very close family. I feel comfortable talking to both of them about anything. However, I find it easier, sometimes, to talk to Daddy-double first before telling my mom something.

I'll tell my stepdad something that I think my mom will get really mad about to see his reaction. If he's like, "Oh, OK," with a smirk on his face, that's when I know it's not that bad for me to tell my mom. She probably won't trip out on me as bad. But if he says, "OK," with no *oh* and then gives me this crazy stare with no smirk, then I think, *Yeah, maybe I shouldn't tell my mom right now. Maybe he will tell her.* It's funny talking about it here in this book, but I be scared for real, ya'll.

You can't just tell my mom something. You have to have a reason for your actions, and it better be good. If not, she will keep talking about it until it makes sense. I think she really should've been a judge or attorney. My mom is going to get to the bottom of the story. And with her, you are guilty until proven innocent.

She does not take sides either. I know, because I have come home to tell my mom about what one of my friends did to me at school, and the first thing she'll say is, "OK, what did you do?" I used to get mad, but I get it. She taught me that just because I am her daughter, that doesn't mean I'm always in the right. Her motto, no matter who it is, is "wrong is wrong, and right is right."

Remember, my mom is the strict parent, and she do not play when it comes to structure, principles, morals, and values.

But I love it. My mom is the reason I am becoming the young lady I am today.

Now, would you like to hear something so heartfelt? On the day my dad passed away, Daddy-double came into the room with me and mom and hugged us both. He said something that made me feel so good inside while hugging us. He said, "Lucious, I promise to take care of them for you. I promise, man."

I thought that was so sweet. It meant a lot for me to hear my stepdad say those words. Ever since that day, my stepdad and I have gotten much closer. We have an amazing father-daughter relationship. I thank God for him coming into our lives.

But real talk, at first, I didn't like him. I didn't like anything he did.

I just felt then like my mom and dad might have a chance to be back together, but not if he was in the way. So, I tried everything to get him out the way. I tried the "Mommy, you act like you love him more than me" card. Then I tried the "Daddy, Daddy, he's being mean to me" card.

This finally ended when my mom called us both into the dining room to sit down and talk. My mom said, "OK, this is not working. Even though I love you and you make me happy, my girls deserves to be happy too. So, at this time, you got—"

Before she could finish, I interrupted (politely, though, since it is my mom we are talking about) and said, "But Mom, it's not Mr. Double. It's me."

You should've seen the look on my mom's face. Well, first, you should've seen the look on his face when she said this wasn't working. I'm not sure if he'd been about to cry, but it had sure looked like it. He'd looked so sad. (Please don't tell him I said this. He doesn't like to show emotions.)

Well, of course, God makes no mistakes. He knew that my mommy needed someone like Daddy-double and that Daddy-double would be great for Colby and me.

Chapter 5: Being Me

I was born in Henry County, Georgia. As far back as I can remember, I always had a good life as a child. My family has always taken great care of me. Some say I am spoiled, but I say I'm just loved a lot.

I didn't understand what was going on with my sister or dad until I was almost four years old. I remember how I used dress up, putting on my mom's heels and wearing her shirt as a dress, and act like I was preaching through the house. I would have my dad, sister, and mom join me in the living room. One day, I got really into it and started going around asking, "What's wrong with that sister right there? Why's she in that wheelchair?" My mom answered, "She can't walk, preacher," so I went over to my sister and put my hands on her. I told my mom and dad to hold hands while I prayed for her. I remember saying, "Lord, heal this sistah. Heal, heal, heal, Lord."

At that time, I didn't know about the Holy Spirit, but I think the Holy Spirit was in me that day.

My mom and dad always told me that I am beautiful, smart, and wise and that I can be whatever I want to be in life, so I should never let anyone or anything stop me. They always tried to warn me about how people are in the world. Some are nice, some are mean, some are happy, and some are sad. As my mom would put it, "Baby girl, always remember, happy people like to make other people happy, and sad people like to make other people sad. So, never take it personally if someone tries to make you sad. Just know that they are not a happy person right now. And if you give them one of your happy smiles, that just might brighten their day." She would also say, "Never look down on anyone, but help those that can't help themselves and pray for everyone."

I really love being me. There were many hard times for me, though, like learning to cope with my dad's disability and having a sister that couldn't walk or talk—not to mention the time I first went to public school.

My mommy wanted me to stay at a private school, but I begged her to please let me go to the public school. I want to be like the other kids and ride the school bus. But, boy, did public school teach me a lesson. And if there's one thing I've learned, it's that not everyone is for you and not everyone is with you. So, I am still working on letting go of my feelings a little bit and not being as sensitive about what others do. Not everyone is going to treat me as I treat them or myself.

I'm not perfect. At all.

Yes, I'm very blessed, but I decided to put this section in because some people and some friends think I'm perfect or am some type of robot that doesn't have feelings just because I may not show them at times.

They judge me from the outside. I live in a nice house. My parents have nice luxury cars. We travel all the time. I wear nice clothes and shoes. Plus my mom gives me these super big birthday parties that my friends get to come to. Again, I am not perfect! And one thing I've really realized is that people don't care as long as it makes them happy. You see, one of my biggest flaws is attachment. I think that once we are friends, we are friends for life—unless, of course, one of us dies. But that's neither here nor there. I expect that my friends will be just as loyal and caring as I am, but I am learning as I get older that that is definitely not the case.

It's been a few months now since my dad passed and only a few people had asked about or even acknowledged the fact that one of the most precious people to me passed away. Most of the people I saw either skipped over asking me how I am doing or acted like my dad had never existed, which both is and isn't OK.

One thing I can say is that my mom has been with me through it all from the time I was born. She was with me when I found out my sister was disabled and when I found out that my dad had diabetes and would never be able to do the fun activities that a dad would usually do with his child. She was with me when I would go to doctor's appointments, on my first day at school, and when I was upset with a friend or someone else. She was there when I lost my dad, and she is still with me now. I thank my mom for being here, not just for me but for my sister too.

But let's get back to the topic. I'm just going to give you an example of how people think I'm perfect or whatever. I have this friend, whose name I won't mention. We went to the same school for about two years, and she told me about how her dad had passed when she'd been four years old. Then we stopped being friends for a few years. Later she asked me if we could be friends again. At first, I was going to say no, because she was being mean and saying bad things about me to other people at the school. But I forgave her and said sure.

I'm not going to keep this part too long, but a few months after we had become friends again, my dad passed away. All she said was, "Oh," and not in a way that made it sound like she was surprised, sympathetic, understanding, or even curious. It was like she didn't care or like she didn't want to know and didn't want me to tell her the story. So, I didn't.

She acted as if she didn't know what it was like to lose a dad. Instead, she started ignoring me and being very rude. I never understood what had happened or why she would act like that, but I realized at an early age that you just have to accept people for who they are and not let what they do or say affect your attitude or love for others.

I find this to be true because when I continue to be kind to people who are not kind to me, God always does something special in my life to show me that I did the right thing. As it says in Ephesians 4:32 (NIV), "Be kind and compassionate to one another, forgiving each other, just as in Christ God forgave you."

In life, there are so many things I'm excited to do, like drive a car, go to college, get my first job, and get my own place, but right now, I'm closest to driving a car and spending my own money than anything else, which is OK.

One thing I have always heard people say is "Ashleigh, you are so blessed to have a life like this and should be grateful for it." And I am so grateful for my life and blessed indeed. But I'm not perfect, and I still have feelings that get hurt.

Now, I don't get into fights with people or get in trouble, because I try to make the right choices. However, I am still human, so I might sometimes make the wrong choice, like not cleaning my room when I should or talking on the phone past my bedtime—the normal teen things you go through.

I love the fact that I have so many great opportunities, but sometimes it can be a lot of work.

I try to keep the end result in mind; that is what keeps me going.

I watch my mom with all she does and have asked her how she can take on so much—work, school, a business, family, friends who depend on her, and being a mom and a wife. She always comes back with "only God."

People always tell me and my mom that we are so alike and that I am a mini her. Sometimes I think I am, but sometimes I don't, because my mom wants to learn more and be more and more active. Pushing myself to be like her has kind of worn me out to where sometimes, I don't even want to do anything (in my silly voice). But I guess that's when I say, I am not perfect.

You know, I started writing this book in January 2020, my dad passed in 2019, and then it happened. Oh boy, I would never have thought things could change so fast. We were faced with this thing called COVID-19. It affected absolutely everything and everybody. The world was literally shut down. This pandemic was really killing my vibe. But we were all trying to stay strong because my family went out all the time. We came up with a lot of cool things to do at home. We put the projector up outside and had movie night. I tried to work out with my mom and Daddy-double, we would go bike riding in the neighborhood, and for family walks every evening. I think I lost probably two or three pounds, which is OK.

Being homeschooled allowed me to focus on myself more.

Since I had become a preteen, I had been struggling with acne. It bothered me a lot. So, I tried a new facial cream to help it go away. I'd first tried using aloe vera straight from the plant on my face, and it had seemed to work. But I didn't use it long enough to see if it really worked. Then I got this face soap from the dermatologist.

That year, I was also getting ready to have headshots taken, which was happening in June. As I mentioned earlier, I had been picked to go to Florida for a big audition for this TV show. This was pretty exciting for me. I was not sure what to expect, but I was really getting better at not being as shy. At least, that's what I thought.

I can say, I was doing more than usual since we were forced to quarantine because of COVID-19.

I was cooking, cleaning, writing, drawing, dancing, singing, learning new things, taking care of Colby, reading, playing a whole lot of Roblox, watching a lot of TV series and movies, and spending time with my family. Honestly, I kind of enjoyed this free time. However, my heart went out to the people out there suffering and dying from this pandemic. I prayed that everything would get better soon in this world.

During quarantine, I didn't have to wake up as early in morning, but I couldn't lie in the bed all morning either, not with my mommy. She believes in getting up and getting it done. Even though we were in this pandemic crisis, my mom still believed that everyone should get up and get dressed. No lying around in our house unless it was the weekend. However, I did get more privileges.

I was getting ready for the big audition in July 2020. I couldn't wait. However, if COVID-19 didn't slow down, we would have to wait until July 2021.

When school started back up, I began attending this online academy. It is a Christian-based school. My mom loved it because I had a Bible class. I liked that part too, but I also liked the fact that you could do your lessons at your own pace—yep, at your own pace—just as long as you got them done. Of course, my mom was always making sure I was not getting too far behind.

Chapter 6: Lights! Camera! Action!

So, there I was, waiting in line with hundreds of people in front of and behind me. I was so nervous at first. I thought, *I can't do this. There are too many people here to compete with.*

After one hour of listening to this guy on the stage talk about how the acting business and film industry works, we finally got up, and hundreds of people got in a line. We were divided by age groups. Each group would go into this room, and then they would shut the door. What! My mind was all over the place. I didn't know what to expect when I got into that room. Now I was really nervous.

It seemed like I stood in line forever. Finally, it was my turn to go in that room, along with some other kids. My heart started beating really, really, really quickly, and I was so scared that I would make a fool of myself or forget a line or even *freeze up*!

I've struggled with social anxiety, especially since my dad passed. I didn't know I had social anxiety at the time, but I would always wonder why I would tense up, start to sweat even though it was really cold, or even have a hard time focusing when I got around a group of people.

I've always wondered how I could have social anxiety if neither of my parents had it. My mom is very outgoing and speaks whatever comes to her mind. My dad was also very outgoing and never had a problem talking or speaking in front of people. I, on the other hand, hate talking in front of people and even just being around people. I know it seems sad, but it's just how some people are.

Anyway, back to the story. So, they had given everyone a small piece of paper with a script on it. Which script it was depended on your age. At the time, I was eleven years old, so I got to play a character from the Disney Channel show *K.C. Undercover*: Judy, the robot girl. If you have seen that show, you know Judy is *sassy*! She has some attitude. When we got into the room, I was excited and less nervous because my parents got to stay with me. My parents sat down along with everyone else. There were about fifty people in there, which was another reason I felt less nervous. It beat being around the hundreds of people in the room where I'd been standing in line.

The same guy who had been on that stage for an hour was now in this room standing in front of everyone. He started calling people's names, and they would come up there and act out the script with him. We started out with a dramatic scene first.

So, this is how it worked: the person auditioning would recite the script from memory, and the guy would say the other lines. The script was set up so that the bolded words were for the auditioning actor to say, while the words not in bold were for the other person to fill in. For example:

The Farm

Greg: Hey! What are you doing?

Jade: Nothing. Getting milk from the cow.

Greg: Good, 'cause I was just about to do it. Thanks, Jade, for doing it.

Jade: Oh! No problem, Greg. I'd thought you needed a bit of help after seeing that long list of things you had to do today.

Now, that was not one of the scripts in the audition. I just made one up really quickly to give you more of a visual. If a girl was auditioning, Greg would be read by the guy—let's just call him Mr. Mike, because I forgot his name and don't want to keep calling him *the guy*. But if you were a boy auditioning, then it would be the other way around. You would be Greg, and Mr. Mike would play the girl, Jade. Now, you can go ahead and feel free to act out the mini script I made. If you don't want to, then continue reading to find out what else is about to happen.

When Mr. Mike called my name, I stood up and walked over in front of the whole room. Mr. Mike started the scene first, and then I said my part. We went back and forth until the scene was over.

I was relieved and still nervous, even after it was over. After everyone had gone, my parents thought I had done a horrible job and were mad at me, but then Mr. Mike said, "If I call your name, stand up." He called the names of about half the people in the room but not mine, so I thought I must not have made it. But then Mr. Mike walked out the room and talked to the people outside. We couldn't hear what he was saying, but we could see through a small, rectangular window in the door. After he got done talking outside, he came back in and said, "Congratulations! You have made it to the second audition."

Everyone was so happy. My parents were in total shock, and honestly, I was too. I couldn't believe I had made it! They told us that the second audition would be even harder than the first, but I thought I was ready. So, the next day, we got in the car and drove downtown to the place they were having the auditions. This time, there were only around forty-five people there. We went into the room, sat down, and Mr. Mike explained everything, saying that if you made it this time, then you were very lucky.

Everyone got their turn. When it was my turn, I froze in the middle of the script. I wasn't scared or nervous; I just went blank and stared at Mr. Mike, even after he was done talking. I was so embarrassed, but I kept going, shook it off, and acted like it hadn't happened.

After my audition was over, my parents were furious. They looked at me like, *What was even the point of coming here? Ashleigh, you didn't even talk loud enough.* I felt bad.

So, Mr. Mike said the same thing he'd said the last time. If he called your name, you were supposed to stand up. He called everyone's name except for three people, including me, and told them all, "Sorry, you did not make it. Please exit out the side door."

My parents and I were thinking, *Wow, some of the best people didn't make it!* Once those people had exited, Mr. Mike congratulated the rest of us who were still there and told us that we had all been picked for Disney Premiere. You should have seen my parents' faces. They were so shocked! They were also happy that I had made it, and that one day I would be on TV.

Inspirational Moment: After my dad passed away, I told my mom that I wanted to be an actor. She told me I could be anything if I put my mind to it. So, I prayed and asked God to bless me to become an actor. And he answered my prayer. Now, I don't know how far it will go, but God truly blessed me with the opportunity. So, I encourage anyone who wants to do something to overcome your fears and just do it.

After we got out of that room, we went into another room, where there were a whole bunch of tables with envelopes on them. Mr. Mike told each family to go sit at a table.

So, my parents and I sat a table and waited for someone to come speak to us about the next step. At first, I had mixed emotions about it. I was feeling happy, joyful, scared, clueless, nervous, and thankful. Mr. Mike went around to each table, talking to each family and congratulating them. Finally, he got to us. Mr. Mike came over with a giant smile on his face and was like, "Congratulations!" And we were like, "Thank you!" Mr. Mike said that I had been picked because he could see the faith in me and could see that I had come from a great home, that I was a brilliant and smart child with a humble spirit, and that I was teachable. He said Disney Premiere needed someone like me. He said that I was a good young actress but that I could be able to get help on the areas I needed help on.

Now let's pause for a minute. Remember when I said I went blank on my line? Yeah, that part. Well, I don't think he knew that, because he even said that he loved how I would pause after I said my line and wait to see if he had something else to say, since most of the other kids just cut him off or talked too long. Then he went on and on about how I would get to meet celebrities from Disney when we went to Disney World, about the different acting levels, and about how the program worked. As we were walking out, the staff said, "Hi! Congratulations! We will see you in Orlando, Florida." And we were like, "Hello! Thank you!"

After we had done everything in that room, we went downstairs and headed out. It was the best night I could ever have asked for at my age. My mom and stepdad were so happy for me.

When we got home, my mom and Daddy-double told me they were proud of me. We talked about plans for going to Orlando and how we would care for Colby. That was the challenging part when we traveled. You see, Colby has a Hoyer lift to lift her at home, but whenever we traveled, my mommy and stepdad would have to lift her themselves.

About a month later, Disney Premiere introduced me to this lady named Alison. She was going to be my coach. She provided me with a script to practice and memorize; the next month, I would act out the script, and Alison would tell me how I did. After that, and all the way up until June, we moved to working on my official scripts. I would have to act out the main script in front of the biggest network people in the industry—at least, that is what we were told. For example, there would be people from the Disney Channel and Nickelodeon. If they saw something they liked during the audition, they could pick us. Very exciting, huh?

If I got picked, I would need an agent, and a whole bunch of other things would change, since I would be a TV or movie star! Well, hopefully. And whether I made it onto a network or not, I would still have an amazing opportunity that I thanked God for. I had been thinking about an opportunity like this all my life. I couldn't give up, because I realized that I was getting older. If I made it, I wouldn't be able to hang out with my friends as much, but I figured I shouldn't sweat that right now. I was one of the three people out of a thousand who had gotten picked; that must have been a sign.

I continued to consistently study and practice my script. My mom and daddy had taught me that when you start something, you finish it. I had come this far with it. Why not give it my best? That's what I do with everything else, like running my own T-shirt business (CS Apparel, LLC), writing this book, helping with my sister, and staying focused in school.

By summer 2021, I had made it! I was honestly very proud of myself. I'd had tough moments and doubts but more faith that anything!

It had been a year and some months since I'd lost my dad. I had new strength each day. I wished that my dad were there to see me now. I was not sad as much, but I still missed him a lot.

I was happy, and my self-esteem level was rising as I came to realize that I was my own person, a beautiful, magnificent, and blessed young lady, and that no one could tell me different! It was summer break, and COVID-19 was somewhat fading away. Most people didn't even wear their masks, and some acted like COVID-19 had never really existed. But my family and I still tried to keep our distance. Anyway, I had just passed sixth grade and was going into seventh that fall. I had been kind of upset that I couldn't do my first year of middle school in an actual school. However, it worked out, because it gave me time to get ready for middle school, like by working on my social anxiety. I was ready now. My best friend and I had been split up and sent to different schools in third grade, I think, so it would be exciting for us to be able to connect at school again.

I hadn't made it to the 2020 audition in Florida because there had been a spike in new COVID-19 infections, but now the moment was finally here. We would be going the next month to Disney World for the big audition! I was really excited, but I still had a lot of mixed emotions about it. I prayed and hoped that I would make it and that the people would really like me. I figured I would probably have to, I don't know, do something that would bring out my personality and help me not be nervous, but whatever happened would happen according to God's plan.

When the time came, the whole family went to hang out in Georgia for four days before we went to Florida, but this is about Florida, so let's stay focused. I had to go to Disney World to do five auditions in front of about four or five different networks. It was very intense but also a great experience. We got there a day early so we could get settled in. The next day, we went to check in and get our schedule; then for the two or three days after that, we practiced in front of our groups. All of us who were auditioning had been split up into groups 5000, 6000, and 7000. Group 5000 was four-to-ten-year-olds, 6000 were eleven-to-thirteen-year-olds, and 7000 were fourteen and older. (I was in the 6000 group.) Every group had a coach that would help us get over our nervousness and help us remember lines and stuff like that.

Finally, the day I'd been waiting for was here. I was very nervous and scared, but I had faith. The first thing we had to do was walk on stage in front of the audience and the agents and just show our personalities, just to give the agents a preview of all the actors. It was kind of like a modeling show.

Afterward, we did a few practice runs, and then we had to line up with our groups and recite our scripts individually. After that, we left the room and met up with our parents, who had not been allowed into the audition room. Some of us, including me, made new friends. That was exciting for me, because I really didn't have any friends besides my best friend. So, it was a really great experience overall! Also, I got a callback from one of the agents there and got picked to be on the next season of a Premiere+ TV show, "*Go Iguanas,*" that was being filmed at the same hotel the following December!

What a blessing! You see, there had been a thousand of us there to audition, but not everyone had gotten this opportunity or even gotten picked by an agent. I really thank and appreciate God for everything! I couldn't have done any of this without God and the support of my family.

I have to say it again. I thank God for everything! And I encourage anyone who is reading this book to trust in him. He will provide for all your needs.

Chapter 7: Can I Just Be Me for a Moment?

So, you're probably wondering why I'm talking about my emotions in this chapter of the book and are probably thinking, *We get it. You have emotions like everyone else.*

Well, that's not the case for me right now. This will help you understand my personality a little more. You see, my emotions, at times, are everywhere.

Sometimes I can be as sensitive as an egg, and other times I can be as tough as rock. Sometimes I'm very sad, and other times I'm very angry. And before I go further into this topic, let me just tell you, no, I'm *not* bipolar! I am a young girl who has had a lot to accept at a young age.

These emotions play a role in how I am feeling at any given time. Sometimes I can be very energetic and bubbly, but not like bells and whistles, because that would be scary, right? Ha ha ha … ha … ha … hen … hen … Sorry about that, ya'll. I was just thinking about clowns, and I have a terrible fear of them. *Ah*! They are so scary.

Getting back on track, I am shy, quiet, caring, spiritual, and fun to be around. I love to draw and write. I have a creative mind and dream of one day coming up with my own fashion or makeup line. I love them both.

I have days when I feel alone, and even though I have a wonderful, loving family, I just don't have good, trusted friends. You see, my whole sixth-grade year, the first year of middle school, took place online because of the pandemic.

The school doors were open! *Yes*! The time was finally here. We would get to return to school, and I was so excited, not only because my best friend and I would be at the same school but also because I would get to experience the whole deal of changing classes, going to my locker, and meeting new friends. Yay! It was all the things that a teenager looks forward to doing. The first couple of weeks were fun. I couldn't wait to go to school. Every day, I was ready to see my friends. But then it happened: the mean kids came out.

Coming from a Christian family of love and compassion for others made me think that everyone was the same. Let's just say I was learning really quickly that it didn't work like that in life. But I had to remember that not everyone had the same type of loving family.

Other people might not get hugged by their parents, have anyone to say "I love you" to them every day, or even get to spend time with their parents. More importantly, they might not even know Jesus.

I understood how it felt to have divorced parents and to lose a parent, but I still knew how to treat people with love.

What I had learned was that Jesus is love and that he wants us to be like him. Reading my Bible from an early age taught me a lot about how to love people even when they don't know how to love you back. That is exactly how Jesus is.

I also found out that not everyone who smiles to your face is genuinely your friend.

There was one girl who wanted to be my friend one minute but not the next. She would ask to be friends again and then go cold and stop talking to me. At first, it bothered me a lot, but I realized that I must protect my heart and not get tied in with people who are not happy or who keep trying to make me unhappy. So, I distanced myself. The emotional roller coaster was not worth my time.

School—more specifically, middle school—is a public environment where different people and opinions are all over. I like middle school, but there are some ups and downs, such as a situation that happened with this boy named Tyren. I'd known him since fifth grade. We were friends then, but we stopped because he would text me inappropriate things, and my mom found out.

Boy, did I get in big trouble! One, I wasn't supposed to be talking to boys on the phone, and two, well, I got *busted*! So, I distanced myself from him in the sixth grade.

Tyren knew my dad had passed, because it had happened during fifth grade and my whole fifth-grade class knew. But one day in seventh grade, Tyren randomly came up to me and asked me in front of my friends and everyone in the lunchroom how my dad had died. He didn't ask in a nice, caring way but in a very unconcerned, mocking sort of way. My new friends hadn't known my dad had passed away because I hadn't wanted people to think I was one of those pick-me girls who wanted people to feel bad for her. It wasn't really their business, so I'd never brought it up.

So, I said to Tyren, "I don't even talk to you anymore. Why are you asking me this?" But he just kept asking me the question. Then he started making up a song to pick at me, singing, "Your dad is dead; your dad is dead," in a laughing voice. At that point, my friend Aya came up and got all in his face, yelling at him, telling him to mind his business, and saying that what he was doing wasn't right. She was undercover cursing him out. And then my guy friends found out, and they told me that they were going to jump Tyren for me because he shouldn't have been messing with me. I tried to tell them that they would get in trouble, but they didn't care. They cornered Tyren in the bathroom and told him that he'd better apologize to me or else. When they all came out, Tyren came over to me and told me he was sorry like four times, so whatever they did, he was sorry. When the school day was over, I had to tell my mom, because she could always tell, for some reason, if I was happy, sad, mad, or holding something back. I got in the car and told my mom, and she was *so* furious at what Tyren had said to me. Now, my school has a parent line for parents to pick up students at the front of the school. My mom literally circled the school parking lot to get back in line three times to go into the school to report him, but each time we got to the entrance, I would convince her not to go in there, because I was OK. She finally agreed but said she would go into school the next day. I tried to convince her not to do anything crazy, because I was scared that she was going to go into the school and find Tyren. (My mom doesn't play about it when it comes to her girls). Now, I thought it would be better when we got home, but like always, my stepdad asked me how my day had been. I told him it had been good aside from when Tyren told me that joke about my dad. I hadn't known Daddy-double could have steam coming out his ears, but he was really mad, and that's exactly what it looked like. So, not only was my mom ready to go up to the school, but now Daddy-double was too. I was trying to calm them down when my mom yelled, "That's it! You're going to a private school." I was like, "Nooooo!" because I actually liked going to a public school. It was just that some people didn't have respect for others, but that's true everywhere you go in life. So, you can imagine the rest of the day at my house. All I could hear was my mom going around the house saying that she was going to my school in the morning and that she would need to contact his parents. I understood why my mom and Daddy-double were upset. Shoot, I was, too, because that was my dad, and I would never want anyone to insult him, make fun of his death, or talk about him in a bad way. I was very upset and mad, but then I realized, that maybe Tyren hadn't gotten the love and affection from his dad that my dad and Daddy-double had given me. So, I learned from that day that people are rude and don't really care what hurts other people. That's why I always pray and ask God to give me strength, and he does. Because of that, I know Jesus loves me.

The next day, my mom, strangely, got in touch with Tyren's dad. You won't believe it, but Tyren's dad was furious. He just could not believe his son had done such a thing. Good thing my mom hadn't gone off when she'd called his dad. Anyway, Tyren's dad was so mad that he made Tyren bring me a gift and a letter of apology. I was very surprised and happy to see it but even happier to hear him say he was sorry and truly mean it this time. I just didn't understand why he'd done that in the first place. Needless to say, we are much better now. He speaks to me, and I speak back. I've had no more problems with him ever since.

Inspirational Moment: "A sweet friendship refreshes the soul and awakens our hearts with joy" (Proverbs 27:9, The Passion Translation).

Chapter 8: What's Happening Now

I had to take a break from writing because of everything I had going on, like school, acting, family, and some me time. Now I'm back, and I'm currently in a good place in life, happy and peaceful! You see, I have learned that you are what you believe in, and as time passes, you will become what you hang around. I've also learned that people come and people go and that you have to be accountable for your actions and the choices you make in life. That's why it is important always to make good choices the first time. That way you won't have to go back and fix what you messed up.

I added this part, because I have learned to be accountable for my own actions and not make excuses. I never give up, I finish what I start, and I work to be the best at whatever I do.

My mom helped me get my own T-shirt business, CS Apparel, LLC (yay!). I have been super busy with it and, may I add, making good money for a beginner. I also got my first credit card last year. This has been a true learning experience, because my mom told me that whatever I make, I need to pay my 10 percent to the Lord first and put 15 percent up in my savings. The remaining I can keep for spending. At first, I was like, wait a minute. This is my money, Mom. I didn't say that to her personally, but that is what I was thinking. I had just picked out some clothes to buy online, but now I had to do *what*?

Ultimately, though, it made me feel good to know that I am growing up and becoming more responsible.

Colby is doing well. She is still smiling and laughing every day, and she is still running the house with her TV and remote control. My mom and stepdad are doing great. If you see them, you will see what true love looks like in a marriage. I love the way they laugh and act silly with each other and with us.

As for how I've been doing with my dad's death, honestly, I still miss him, because he'll always have a special place in my heart. Still, I'm handling it very well. I just had to realize that people come and go and that God does things for a reason. I'm not saying that he took my dad to upset my family or me, but I read a devotion a while back that said that God plans your life way before you are born! So, I have accepted that. And God knew I would not be angry at him or upset because he took someone dear from me. Maybe it happened for a reason I don't know now but will understand later in life.

Right now, I understand that I loved and love my dad and that he will always love me. I know that he is in a better place watching over me! Sometimes I get teary-eyed and even cry, because I miss him, but it's OK, because if I didn't cry sometimes, that would be weird and concerning.

Other than that, I have started getting into social media and discovering different things, like TikTok, Instagram, Twitter, and a lot of influencers, but that stuff is not that important.

I'm actually pleased right now and doing well with being more confident. I've learned how to speak up in public. I started by just saying my order while sitting at a restaurant. Then, I worked on talking to other people when I'm out if I need to know directions or something. Now I've learned how to speak loudly and clearly and stay self-motivated.

I'm also starting to figure out my career path and what I want to be when I get older. I enjoy acting and would like to see how far it will go. My goal is to make it onto a Netflix series. Once I accomplish that, I want to produce and direct my own movie. Those are my dreams and goals right now! There are several celebrities from Netflix shows who I admire and would love to meet, like Ian Somerhalder. I really like him, and not just because of his good looks! I love his personality and humor. He is an actor who was on one of my favorite Netflix series, *The Vampire Diaries*.

I also want to meet Nina Dobrev, who is one of my idols. She is honestly a really great actress. She was also on *The Vampire Diaries*. There are many other people I would love to meet as well.

I also want to go to college and become an attorney because I feel that I'm really good at getting my point across and helping others see points of view different than their own.

I know I can make it and will succeed in whatever I want to do by praying and keeping faith in God. Also, I must put the work into it as well. Some people forget to do that last part.

So, my friend, I encourage you to always put God first in everything you do. You can be it and do it, so don't lose hope. And if you lose a loved one, I encourage you to keep living. Don't get stuck in the same place. Your loved one would want to see you happy. Remember also, when you see someone who is disabled, don't overlook the individual. He or she needs love and attention too. Finally, for those who are struggling with self-esteem issues, you are beautiful and smart. Never let anyone tell you anything different. Love yourself and know that you are loved!

Chapter 9: Life's Way

Inspirational Moment: I called this book *In Life There Is a Way!* because there always is a way in life. You just have to find the right path. I really want to find my purpose in life, and I want to know why I am here. Why did God put me in this position, this scenario, in life? So, over the years, I've been trying to get closer to God to see what my purpose is in life. I even try new things to see if I would like to pursue them. Right now, maybe you've been trying to choose a college or the profession you want to pursue when you get out of college. That's how it is for me currently. I enjoy acting for Premiere+, and I think this is the right way to go right now, but my long-term goal is to be an attorney. However, life can be overwhelming and stressful at times. That's why I feel that it is good always to pray and talk to God about which direction to go.

When I say "life's way," I mean that life has its way. Things happen for a reason. We can do things differently and still get the same outcome. No matter what happens in life, the result will be the same because that is the path God planned for you. However, our choices could delay or affect God's plan for our lives. Therefore, I encourage you not to be upset with God when life takes another turn than expected. Sometimes it just means God is preparing you and mending you for something better in life. That's why I thank God every day for everything and for the things he has done for me and is going to do for me. Even though it has been difficult having a disabled sister and losing my father, along with other things I have encountered, I've always kept my head held high because, in the end, in life, there's a way.

"For I know the plans I have for you," declares the Lord, "plans to prosper you and not to harm you, plans to give you hope and a future."

—Jeremiah 29:11 (NIV)

I hope that you enjoyed reading my book and that your life will be truly blessed!

Printed in the United States
by Baker & Taylor Publisher Services